**This book is the fruit of many years of practitioners'
field research.
For any issues with your book, such as
faulty binding, printing errors, or something else.
Please, do not hesitate to contact us at:
fajrour@gmail.com
We will make sure you get a replacement copy
immediately.**



For any suggestions or questions regarding our books,
Contact us at:  fajrour@gmail.com

Please, support us and leave a   review
Thank you!

# Table of contents

when you hear the word contemplation, you most likely think a Hindu spiritual and ascetic discipline "Yoga". That is on the grounds that for quite a while, or possibly in the course of recent decades, contemplation has essentially been proceeded as the way of specific bodily postures, widely practiced for health and relaxation.

In any case, contemplation, doesn't generally have anything to do with Yoga. It is in reality a demonstration in itself. Reflection is commonly performed in the wake of doing Yoga practice, since it drives you into a condition of quiet, which is ideal for contemplation. meditation is a very sensitive field of research, yet practitioners try to clarify the key purposes of reflection and why it ought to be rehearsed.

Above all, a large number of us have confusions about reflection. The most well-known misinterpretation is that reflection is tied in with disposing of thought! That would set anybody up for disappointment! Reflection, rather, is tied in with turning into the onlooker of thought instead of the reactor to thought. According to Andreson (2000), meditation has certainty endured 4500 years of political change and financial progress.

The word meditation generally disarrays a portion of individuals because of it being obscure or viewed as fairly supernatural, new age, or connected with an extraordinary creed or religion. In fact, there is nothing surprising about contemplation and I accept that the establishment for reflection in its immaculateness isn't confounding or complex. The very embodiment of meditation is straightforwardness. I truly accept this announcement to be exact in particularly western culture's lifestyle.



I suppose that you have at any point been in stunningness at a wonderful nightfall. To such an extent that you overlooked what happened five minutes prior, and you weren't contemplating what's to come? You were totally at the time and had this feeling of aliveness inside? All things considered, that is reflection!

Meditation is the act of concentrating on a particular item or a solitary purpose of mindfulness. It is the act of quieting the brain to permit one to become drenched with their actual substance; the genuine self that is unified with all (source, the universe, divine awareness, all-inclusive cognizance or some other given name meaning the equivalent).

practitioners talk about heaps of ways to deal with contemplation; several distinct tips and methods. These all work; unquestionably first and foremost they help to center your focus. It is, notwithstanding, significant not to get connected to a specific procedure or item. Regardless of anything else reflection is about a post acknowledgement that you have found the mystery hole that is depicted as nothingness, void, nonexistence.

At exactly this point you have to deeply think that the key concept isn't to get a handle on what you have found, however, essentially permit it to be, converging with the quietness, and the serenity that is the unadulterated embodiment of our universe. In his book, "What Is meditation?", Loot Nairn alludes to reflection as a condition of "exposed consideration." He clarifies, "It is a profoundly alert and dexterous perspective since it expects one to remain mentally present and 'with' whatever occurs in and around one without adding to or taking away from it in any capacity." Accordingly, we may focus on:

• The act of preparing one's psyche to center or going into a profound degree of cognizance of oneself, increasing a comprehension of the equivalent, with or without the desire for some advantage, is contemplation.

• Reflection on a very basic level requires arrangement of the brain conception and body (and soul) so as to accomplish an increased feeling of self being. It requires isolating the outer world from the inward one and concentrating just on the center.

• Meditation has been rehearsed long times ago, in strict, profound and wellbeing rehearses. It's anything but a determination from any  of them. Every one of these practices gets some type of advantage from reflection.

3-Religion and meditation

Meditation existed before history was recorded. Archaeologists discovered antiquated Indian sacred texts which point the act of reflection going back a great many years. It is an all-around recorded act of numerous world religions to incorporate Buddhism, Christianity, Hinduism, Islam, Jainism, Judaism, Sikhism and Taoism. Spreading from the East, reflection and meditation methods are currently exercised all through the world by a huge number of individuals regularly. The physical act of yoga, through the road of the breath, is in itself a moving reflection which again is rehearsed by a large number of individuals all through the world.

Different religions use contemplation as a piece of firm practices since it has numerous constructive outcomes on the individuals who practise it in different ways. Hinduism, Buddhism, Islam, Christianity are a portion of the significant religions on the planet, that spread the significance of contemplation. Particularly if there should be an occurrence of Buddhism, where Gautama Buddha discovered edification through reflection. Reflecting to the Om serenade in Hinduism (Dhyana), is a notable work on during functions. Additionally, in Islam, Dhikr is a reflective practice among spiritualists in Sufism. The Spinning Dervishes of the Mevlevi Request, are additionally viewed as in a profound daze, a type of profound reflection.

In religion, reflection is rehearsed as a strategy for concentrating on the custom and on the inner human being. That is, contemplation is done so as to discover inward harmony, condition of unity and arrangement of the brain, body and soul.

Otherworldliness and reflection have an exceptionally profound association, for the most part in light of the fact that both try to accomplish a similar reason. Inward harmony and increased feeling of being to absolutely reach an adequate human balance.

## 4-Health and meditation

There isn't a lot of need to expound on this one. We're all acquainted with yoga and reflection. Reflection can quiet down the whole body and manage all the procedures. The attention being all together on loosening up the body does some incredible things and fix inner problems.

Indeed, even an insignificant five to ten minutes of centered daily meditation, can help mend a great deal of intense subject matters, issue like uneasiness and discouragement are additionally controlled through it.

meditation has numerous medical advantages. Strangely, an expanded capacity to focus permits the individuals who experience the ill effects of interminable torment to facilitate their agony by deciding not to concentrate on it. It can likewise help with different other medical issues, including nervousness, misery, stress, a sleeping disorder, HIV/Helps and malignant growth. It can likewise upgrade the body's safe framework, making us more averse to become ill.

Studies have likewise indicated that contemplation can assist with turning around the coronary illness. In the diary Stroke, 60 African/Americans experiencing a solidifying of the supply routes were approached to contemplated for 6-9 months. The individuals who ruminated demonstrated a remarkable reduction in the thickness of their corridor dividers. The individuals who didn't think demonstrated an expansion in thickness. The ends were very sensational. Reflection offers a potential 11% lessening in danger of a having a respiratory failure, and 8-15% decline in danger of having a stroke.

## 5- How to Choose a Meditation strategy

Be that as it may, with such a large number of various strategies for reflection accessible, how can one pick a reasonable, compelling meditation strategy for oneself or one's family? Here are some timesaving tips from long-lasting meditators and reflection instructors to assist you with assessing which contemplation may be best for you.

The initial step is to perceive that not all meditation procedures are the equivalent. The different reflection rehearses connect with the psyche in various manners. Vipassana, known as care reflection, underlines impartial perception and, in it' s increasingly philosophical structure, the examination of temporariness, now and again concentrating on the interconnection among psyche and body. Buddhist practices are probably going to utilize fixation, regardless of whether coordinated at one's breath.

The Supernatural meditation procedure utilizes easy regard for experience unobtrusive conditions of thought and by utilization of a particular mantra. Christian Focusing Supplication utilizes an expression of love to invigorate responsiveness to God. Furthermore, this is just a little testing of the assortment of practices ordinarily lumped together as 'meditation and reflection.'

Various methods have various purposes, utilize an assortment of techniques and normally produce various outcomes. In figuring out which procedure among this wide assortment of practices may best suit your motivations, start by soliciting yourself what you need out from meditation, and how much time you're willing to give it. Some contemplation programs underline normal or twice-every day practice after some time to increase most extreme profit and advance to higher phases of self-improvement, while different practices are planned for a periodic persuasive lift or to chill when you're pushed.

Another inquiry to pose to yourself: do you need a meditation practice that accompanies a religion, reasoning or lifestyle? Numerous practices are entwined into a calculated world view that is a many-sided portion of the training whether it's a methodology that mulls over the universe and human brain as indivisible components of a solitary request, or a world view that endeavours to get past all creed and consider them to genuinely seem to be, it's as yet another intellectually imagined world view. Different practices, for example, the type of care meditation now famous in the West, or the Supernatural Reflection procedure, are common in nature and can be drilled without grasping a specific way of thinking, religion or lifestyle.

It is safe to say that you are looking to accomplish motivation and bits of knowledge during the reflection experience. Reflections that fall into this classification are scrutinizing procedures. They guarantee more prominent profundity of comprehension about the theme being considered and help the acumen comprehend different roads of thought. These sorts of reflections can be lovely and genuinely elevating, particularly if there is no stressing or psyche control included.

## 6- Types of Meditation

Meditation has numerous advantages. It has been logically demonstrated to deliver noteworthy advantages both for body and soul in the individuals who use it as part of their daily activities. Along these lines, an ever-increasing number of individuals are figuring out how to ponder to exploit this colossal fundamental ability.

As the pace of life increments and the anxieties gather, reflection offers an adequate shelter from social pressure and madness of the world. At the point when you ponder, you improve your passionate prosperity. This is one of the most notable advantages of contemplation. Individuals who think about a customary premise are more settled and more joyful in general. Reflection has been demonstrated to lessen the force of sorrow and limits the impact of uneasiness, making it a significant emotional well-being apparatus.

Additionally, individuals improve their physical prosperity when they contemplate. Studies showed that Individuals who meditate all the more normally have lower pulses and lower circulatory strain estimations. A few people have begun pondering as an approach to lessen or wipe out their pulse drug and make themselves more beneficial.

Different kinds of meditation are in use today. This assortment has originated from a long convention of reflection, extending back a huge number of years. As these customs develop and form and come into the advanced time, there have been expanded varieties and modifications to make them increasingly open to current crowds. However, the fundamental framework has not changed.

## 6.1 Guided meditation

Guided meditation is perhaps the most straightforward type of reflection around. In this framework, there are verbal prompts given ceaselessly all through the whole contemplation time frame. This is particularly basic in meditation rehearses intended to deliver a particular impact, similar to reflection for rest or reflection for stress alleviation.

## 6.2 Centred breathing

Centred breathing is one of the most famous kinds of meditation. In this method, you tally your breaths and check a particular number of beats as you take in and afterwards consider the beats you inhale out. This powers you to have a long, consistent inhale, which fills a few needs. To start with, it compels you to coordinate your concentration and limits interruptions. Second, long customary breaths bring down your pulse and help unwinding.

## 6.3 Mantras

Mantras are a notable meditation method. These are things you state - or even think- over and again as you ruminate. The "om" is, obviously, the principal thing that everybody considers when they hear the word mantra, yet there are some more. Keep in mind that anything that keeps you concentrated on your reflection and liberated from interruptions is a substantial mantra.

## 6.4 Explicit things

Numerous meditators attempt to concentrate on explicit things. For instance, you may attempt to concentrate on a piece of your body, similar to your lower leg, or you may concentrate on a particular spot. This is one motivation behind why numerous individuals ponder in a spot with candles, on the grounds that looking at the fire can help in your core interest.

## 6.5 Strolling reflection

One more of the numerous sorts of contemplation that are accessible to new meditators is strolling reflection. In this procedure, you walk gradually, concentrating completely on the development of your body as you step forward. By concentrating on your means and your breathing you make an engaged outlook that guides your contemplation.

Strolling meditation shouldn't be solely strolling, any type of development will work. A few people like to do their moving contemplation with different exercises. All things considered, normal, cadenced exercises work best. Swimming is one model, as you can concentrate on each stroke being a similar length and speed. A few people likewise prefer to join contemplation with yoga.

## 6.6 Care rehearses

Care rehearses offer individuals the chance to transform each day by day activity into reflection. At the point when you are careful with your activities, every second is a chance to discover internal harmony and tranquillity. This is propelled work and is hard for amateurs. Some would state it's a battle for all individuals, yet by permitting your brain all things considered and concentrating on every second for itself, your whole day can be a reflection.

## 6.7 Gathering method

Pondering with a gathering is famous. Bigger urban communities frequently have one or even a few reflection bunches that meet to think together. This can help apprentice meditators on the grounds that they have the help of a gathering and a customary opportunity to rehearse, which can support consistency. These gatherings are frequently simple to discover and meet a few times each week to make it simple for individuals to go along with them.

## 6.8 Loneliness method

A few people lean toward sorts of meditation that are done alone. These individuals regularly decide to ruminate in their own home and find that contemplation is best experienced as a lone procedure. Numerous individuals ruminate before anything else so as to clear their brain before they face the day ahead.

Contemplation can assist you with unwinding before bed, so you rest better. This is a well-known opportunity to contemplate and sleep time reflection is quite often a lone interest. By clearing your brain and soul from the anxieties and uneasiness of the day you simply finished, you can meet the night with a fresh start which will assist you with resting quicker, rest better and have better dreams.

Every one of these kinds of reflection can assist you in finding your enthusiastic focus. In the event that you are keen on exploring different avenues regarding contemplation, there are numerous things you can attempt. Attempt all the various types of reflection that intrigue you so as to guarantee that you discover one that suits you best.

For some, individuals, beginning with guided contemplation is most effortless, however, you can likewise try different things with centered breathing, work with mantras, attempt a mobile or moving reflection strategy or concentrate on a light's fire. Regardless of what you attempt, contemplation makes certain to improve a mind-blowing nature.

## 6.9 Effective method to Meditate

Meditation is tied in with giving up and to find the mystery key you need to release everything. Relinquish any result before you start. Numerous meditation methods are used today all over the world. Notice that a more than a huge number of years diverse reflection rehearses have advanced. The genuine substance of reflection, be that as it may, is simply to sit and be. Simply you are going past the 'moulded' mind and lifting your brain to a condition of unadulterated mindfulness.

While you can concentrate on an article or on your breath to assist you with reaching this state, at last, it is a characteristic procedure which develops after some time, the pith ought to consistently be in associating yourself with your source. You are searching internally without really endeavouring to do anything besides to simply sit and be.

It is additionally viable to ruminate over specific inner and physical battles or issues we are encountering in our lives. For example, in the event that we need to go to a choice on a specific part of our life; a lifelong heading, for instance, thinking about this can assist us with arriving at the appropriate response. Now and again the appropriate responses we are looking for can come into our psyches very quickly. The intensity of centering fixation and coordinating that concentration towards a specific inquiry or subject can create astonishing outcomes.

It is a smart thought to have a reflection space. This can be a room or part of your home where you feel generally great. You may have delicate lighting, candles, incense, pads, blossoms, and different articles which summon sentiments of quiet and unwinding.

## 7- Basic standards

The entire idea of meditation takes on different characters depending on what a person's goal is while playing out a picked contemplation. Some may need physical or mental help, others, answers or headings for a superior life. In any case, decisions are plainly individualized. Discover yours since this goes far in helping you along the way supported with a one of a kind, customized reason. Characterize it for you! To start a reflection, a couple of basic standards are all around acknowledged. These are:

Split away from interruptions. Mood kills the outside electrical/mechanical interruptions like telephones, PCs, television's and so on. A tranquil, quiet serene spot is liked. From the outset, submit ten minutes or more with no interference.

The stance is significant in that you should be agreeable. Ideally, this is with your back upstanding and your spine to your head straight. Typically, a situated situation on the ground is favoured with hands in your lap; it should likewise be possible in a seat. Resting at first isn't proposed as your body can expect a rest mode.

Close your eyes delicately, loosen up your jaw and facial muscles. Do a "body check" searching for any muscle pressure that may exist discharging any found. Keep loosening up now for a couple of seconds permitting your body to get settled. Be perceptive of a substantial strain emerging. The key is to truly unwind.

Gradually empty your lungs totally. Delicately breathe in and breathe out through your noses with a profound from the midsection musical cycle completely filling your lungs and ousting the air totally. Slow, long in and out-breaths are perfect. Stopping quickly toward the finish of each in and out-breath. Concentrate on the inclination and sounds during the whole cycle.

Enact the heart-mind association which gives an underlying idea clearing mode. Try not to endeavour to smother these musings. Recognize them. Quickly as considerations emerge, excuse them by encompassing any with the six-heart ethics of: gratefulness, empathy, absolution, modesty, valour, and comprehension. Another amazing strategy is to apply genuine love, without a judgment position, to any considerations that may emerge, discharge them and return center to your relaxing.

Consistently and gradually increment the time length spent in your training. As the snapshots of time protract between emerging meditation, you are currently well while in transit to more elevated levels of reflection. Remind yourself to see and value the useful side-effects you have recovered.

## 8-Advantages of meditation and reflection

The tranquillity of psyche, improved fixation and center, uplifted clearness, expanded imperativeness and revival, joy and enthusiastic dependability, improved memory and learning capacity, inward harmony, quiet and unity are only a portion of the advantages ordinary act of reflection can give you.

There have been numerous examinations worldwide that demonstrate contemplation and profound breathing to be gainful. The impacts and advantages become progressively articulated and significant in total, as the training expands on itself. Simply realize that the advantages have been appeared to help with hypertension, a sleeping disorder, discouragement, uneasiness, dietary problems, torment the board, and even symptoms of malignant growth medicines, just as habit and recovery.

Some meditation educators urge individuals to frame a network of a couple of individuals who can ruminate together. Guided reflection classes are accessible everywhere. Yoga studios frequently have yoga classes or guided meetings, as do numerous schools and places of love. For fledglings, ruminating with a gathering can be informational, charming, and simpler than beginning alone.

Simply recollect, there is no specific approach to contemplate. Make the wisest decision to you. You'll possibly do it consistently in the event that it sounds good to you and feels better. Where you do, only it or with individuals, the hour of day or night, music or no music, sitting or resting - go with your senses and emotions. Whatever works best, will be ideal.

Find meditation and the mystery key and you will open an entryway associating you to your actual self, your spirit, and driving you down the way of self-acknowledgement; that you are unified with the universe, some portion of the entire that is all over the place, everybody and everything.

The least complex things are regularly the hardest to fathom. Reflection is the key that opens the entryway to your spirit, who you truly are, your motivation, why you are here and the genuine significance of life. It is your duty to find the key and to use it properly. Start your own journey and find meditation for yourself.

It is the way to all ponder and the entryway to the embodiment of everything. It must be found inside, by converging with the quiet, the quietness and the peacefulness of the body and soul. We have to find the way to meditation and the mystery hole that prompts an existence of satisfaction, bliss, and all-out inward harmony. Life gets streaming, easy, and excellent and simultaneously you accomplish mindfulness which brings clearness, inventiveness and a profound feeling of the genuine reason that is essentially simply being. Here's a short rundown of the advantages that originate from a day by day reflection practice:

• Builds new dimensions to focus on human inner capacities

• Generates a clear and quiet life

• Successfully diminish worry in your life

• Encourages mental prosperity and discharges pressure

• Builds energy and brings a feeling of quiet

• Loosens up the body and brain

 • Brought down of your circulatory strain

• Brings down danger of hypertension and different pressure issue

• Makes congruity of brain and body

 • prompts higher/positive vitality


The rushing about regular daily existence is stifling our brains of the harmony we merit. Our innovation progressions shouldn't choke out our brains; it ought to permit us to accomplish more harmony. Contemplation helps put those occasions in context for our day by day errands.

Science has demonstrated that meditation brings down the circulatory strain, which consequently is identified with your feelings of anxiety and stresses the executives. Obviously superior to taking pills to bring down your circulatory strain. Besides, Normal reflection prompts higher/positive vitality that you are reliably taking advantage of. This successfully makes you lovely to be near, and individuals like that also.Individuals normally incline toward the individuals who cause them to feel great. Otherworldly mindfulness is fortified with an everyday meditation practice. You normally become increasingly mindful of your environmental factors, and higher mindfulness consistently prompts a more profound association with positive matters.

Studies have indicated that contemplation mitigates the negative impacts of pressure, uneasiness and sadness. Generally speaking, we become more settled, more joyful and increasingly satisfied.

Reflection improves focus, which is basic to understanding our actual potential. Centred fixation produces extraordinary force and when our forces of focus are improved, we can utilize this to contemplate as well as in our different drills as well. Some portion of accomplishing our objectives and wants is being able to ace our considerations. By quieting the brain and centering our focus, we can encounter this self-dominance and we can start to change and supplant our negative or undesirable musings with positive ones. This move-in our manner of thinking adjusts our vitality to that of general vitality vibrations and we will start to see positive changes and upgrades all through all aspects of our lives.

Genuinely reflection diminishes pressure-related side effects, for example, heart palpitations, strain and headache migraines, upset rest and bad dreams and despondency. As stress and nerves are diminished, we are really diminishing the likelihood of encountering any heart-related diseases.

Studies have additionally demonstrated that reflection can assuage constant agony, drop cholesterol levels and improve the circulatory strain. The progression of air to the lungs increments and improves and we will encounter a general more prominent feeling of prosperity.
Contemplation benefits our brains too. It instructs us to more readily control our considerations. This enables us to calm those pestering negative considerations we may have every once in a while. A recent report, on mental preparing influences and restricted mind assets in PLOS Science, proposes that meditation practice prompts longer capacities to focus.

## 9- Fantasies about meditation

Practitioners tend to correct people misconception. They showed that meditation isn't focus, however de-fixation. It is the act of discharging one's psyche of all pointless data. The thought is to concentrate on overlooking the outer components. Besides, meditation isn't at all a strict practice. It is utilized in ceremonies. Contemplation has nothing to do with religion or convictions of a specific religion. There is no such association.

Reflection is in certainty for the youthful! Contemplation destresses and keep up a feeling of quiet. This is most basic when we are youthful and managing the weights of work and different exercises. Almost certainly the old profit by contemplation. Yet, it is the youngsters who truly need it.

## 10 - Meditation and mind targets

There is a typical belief that meditation must be used in a totally quiet condition, with your eyes shut, situated with a certain goal in mind. This is completely false. Meditation should be possible whenever of the day, anyplace you are and you can do it with your eyes fully open.

Recall the thought is to close out the outside world and spotlight on yourself. What preferable route over to do it in outright turmoil. Individuals who practice contemplation in places where there are some measures of disturbance, become unquestionably increasingly skilled at controlling their brains.

Meditation opens up new horizons and encourages you to get yourself and that makes you progressively open to the world. You don't turn into a hermit; an incredible inverse. As much as I might want to continue onward, this point is too huge to even think about ending unexpectedly early. In any case, the above essentials on reflection should assist you with getting a screenshot of the bigger picture to start your personal meditation journey.

## 11- Daily dose for positive meditation

The entire idea of meditation takes on different characters depending on what a person's goal is while playing out a picked contemplation. Some may need physical or mental help, others, answers or headings for a superior life. In any case, decisions are plainly individualized. Discover yours since this goes far in helping you along the way supported with a one of a kind, customized reason. Characterize it for you! To start a reflection, a couple of basic standards are all around acknowledged. These are:

Split away from interruptions. Mood kills the outside electrical/mechanical interruptions like telephones, PCs, television's and so on. A tranquil, quiet serene spot is liked. From the outset, submit ten minutes or more with no interference.

The stance is significant in that you should be agreeable. Ideally, this is with your back upstanding and your spine to your head straight. Typically, a situated situation on the ground is favoured with hands in your lap; it should likewise be possible in a seat. Resting at first isn't proposed as your body can expect a rest mode.

Close your eyes delicately, loosen up your jaw and facial muscles. Do a "body check" searching for any muscle pressure that may exist discharging any found. Keep loosening up now for a couple of seconds permitting your body to get settled. Be perceptive of a substantial strain emerging. The key is to truly unwind.

Gradually empty your lungs totally. Delicately breathe in and breathe out through your noses with a profound from the midsection musical cycle completely filling your lungs and ousting the air totally. Slow, long in and out-breaths are perfect. Stopping quickly toward the finish of each in and out-breath. Concentrate on the inclination and sounds during the whole cycle.

Enact the heart-mind association which gives an underlying idea clearing mode. Try not to endeavour to smother these musings. Recognize them. Quickly as considerations emerge, excuse them by encompassing any with the six heart ethics of: gratefulness, empathy, absolution, modesty, valour, and comprehension. Another amazing strategy is to apply genuine love, without a judgment position, to any considerations that may emerge, discharge them and return center to your relaxing.

Consistently and gradually increment the time length spent in your training. As the snapshots of time protract between emerging meditation, you are currently well while in transit to more elevated levels of reflection. Remind yourself to see and value the useful side-effects you have recovered.

Dawn and nightfall are the best occasions of day for meditation on the grounds that our psyches are increasingly responsive on these occasions. Dawn is the beginning of another day and wherever hushes up, quiet and tranquil. The day has not yet started and following a peaceful rest, our psyches will, in general, be more quiet. At dusk, the day is consummation and contemplation as of now empowers us a calm reflection on the day we have recently passed. Our psyches are slowing down as of now before resting, and the quietness that reflection carries will be with us as we float off to rest, helping us to feel revived and stimulated when we stir the next morning.

Spot a pad on the floor and seat yourself with the goal that your base is half on and half off the pad. This will hoist your hips and normally lift your spine and you will feel better than if you were simply sitting on the floor. Bring yourself into a leg over leg position. Generally, the lotus or half-lotus present is utilized while contemplating however in the event that you can't easily sit in these postures, sit as is directly for you. Leave your spine alone upstanding and tilt your head with the goal that your eyes, when open, are fixed three feet before you. Spot your hands any place they feel good; one on the other in your lap, in a mudra with the tip of the thumb contacting the tip of the first or center finger to frame a circle, or just spot them on your thighs. Whatever is agreeable and feels directly for you.

There are numerous things you can concentrate on during reflection; sculptures, blossoms or a solitary rose, silk scarves, candles, precious stones, music, mantras and the breath to give some examples. Examine yourself with each of these and find what works best for you.

As anyone might expect I have seen the easiest techniques as the best; the breath and a mantra. The model I have utilized all through a large portion of this area is the breath, which is by a wide margin the most all-inclusive focal point of meditation.

Close your eyes and start to concentrate on your breath. Concentrate on each breath in and breathe out. Quietly saying the words 'SO' on the breath in and 'Murmur' on the breath out additionally helps center. Permit your considerations to travel every which way however consistently return your concentration to your breath. On the off chance that you have picked an article, you would just concentrate on that item permitting the contemplations to travel every which way restoring your concentration to the item. After sometimes, meditation gets simpler and you will discover as your self-dominance develops you are effectively ready to sit for 20-30 minutes.

In any case, simply take a shot at accomplishing ten minutes two times every day and afterwards increment to fifteen, etc. Contemplation can be viable whenever. On the off chance that you can't ruminate routinely locate some peaceful time when you can to permit yourself to just sit and be. Focus on your breath and imagine yourself sitting in some places which will help achieve a without a care in the world perspective. One of my top choices is on a seashore before a delightful quiet blue ocean. Pick something which feels right and valid for you. Be persistent and delicate with yourself. As your capacity to ruminate expands, your degree of mindfulness develops. You will start to see enhancements with every day's contemplation practice.

Permit yourself to turn into your own quiet observer and essentially watch the breath. As you follow each breath in and breathe out, contemplations will turn out to be slower and slower. Allow the musings to come and let them go, just watching them and not getting appended to them. Your center is the breath, consistently come back to the cadenced breath in and breathe out. At this point permit yourself to turn into the breath. With this consolidating comes discharge and without a genuine flashing acknowledgement, you are drenched in tranquillity, in the quiet and you have found the mystery key to open new horizons. This is the spot of being, of the essence and of your actual self. Here you are at one with all the fixings; regardless of whether that be the universe, Tao, awareness or whatever your term for it is, you are it, it is you and it and you are everything.

There is a consensus that meditation is an excursion of self-disclosure that prompt self-dominance that you can begin at the present time - today. There is nothing you have to discover that you don't have directly right now inside you. Basically, sit and permit yourself to be. It is difficult, preparing the frantic mind that races to start with one idea then onto the next at the same time, with training, it turns into an inviting chance to invest energy with yourself.

A contemplation educator can help and guide you through the act of reflection and going to a gathering meditation meeting will empower you to impart the experience to other people, which can support your own training. Nonetheless, I would ask you to begin rehearsing yourself as I have portrayed in this segment. There is nothing a reflection instructor can disclose to you that you don't as of now have any acquaintance with, you simply need to sit and be with yourself to find it.

Quietness isn't something we regularly experience every day or even greeting so far as that is concerned. A great many people think that it is exceptionally hard to truly unwind and give up due to some personal specific considerations. The significant point to recollect is that you are making an effort not to drive your contemplations away, however just permitting them to be, without connection to them. This training after sometimes lessens the number of considerations, and interruptions, you experience during reflection. Numerous individuals' lives are occupied and feverish with work responsibilities, money related weights, parenthood, mingling, side interests, premiums and an entire rundown of different exercises that take up most within recent memory.

Settle on a cognizant choice to make time to ruminate. Focus on leaving on your own excursion of self-disclosure. Open your own extraordinary innovative potential which, with proceeded with the training of meditation, will be unbounded.

## 13- Meditation journey

There is a typical misguided judgment, that contemplation was a fairly mysterious practice that assumed control over your body and brain by one way or another, that it was something to be dreaded nearly and it was just truly polished by priests and spiritualists. I was unable to have been all the more off-base!

Meditation is just the passage to the spirit, the vehicle to convey you more profound entity into yourself and a training strategy that opens up a piece of you that has consistently existed, however, that you never acknowledged was there; your actual self and that which gives you the genuine significance of your reality and interconnectedness to the universe and everybody and everything else in it.

Without reflection, I would not be the glad and satisfied individual I am today. It has empowered me to find progressively about myself, to understand my actual potential on numerous levels in any case, in particular, revealed the pot of gold toward the finish of the rainbow, that which individuals look for and frequently feel they never find. It is the finished and immaculate unity; the information that we are each of the one, some portion of the entire that is the universe and past, that which is only that which is everything. Attempt to get it and it is no more. The excellence of this acknowledgement brings numerous things; internal harmony, inward quiet and serenity, significant clearness and a profound feeling of having a place, of direction and of genuine delight. That is the essence of life, the genuine significance of life.

I think the explanation such a large number of individuals never discover this or find this is on the grounds that they are searching for something outer. They look for bliss and satisfaction through realism, connections, employments, occasions, cash, etc. They miss what is as of now there, effectively ideal similarly for what it's worth, directly before them, and just by giving up and totally giving up to it do you become it. This is the thing that the Buddha implied when he said by the nonappearance of getting a handle on one is liberated.

I have not reached my utmost capacity since that would mean there is a limit to my latent capacity. My potential capacity is vast thus I appreciate the progression of life and trust totally toward the path that takes. Of course, I make expectations and make what I might want to bring into my life however I additionally believe that everything that comes into it is by one way or another piece of my excursion, my life exercises, thus I am continually gaining from it. I am simply me and I am likewise you, the universe and everything in it. My motivation is to help other people accomplish their own self-acknowledgement and start their own trip. The excursion starts past the entryway that prompts your spirit; your actual self and reflection is the way to opening that entryway.

My day by day reflection and meditation practices, which is as a rule for an hour every morning, resembles energizing my entire framework. It resembles getting back to where I originated from. It's allowing me to completely relinquish the dualistic reality we live in and enter a world that you can't see or contact however that through your heart you know is consistently there at whatever point you should wish to be there. It stimulates, washes down and renews your psyche and body from the back to front. It resembles plunging inside yourself and turning out to be one that is basically non-presence, nothingness, however yet that which is everything and all over the place. This is the genuine significance of discovering paradise on earth.

The drenching of self-being in the quietness gives extraordinary force and vitality, energizing the entire framework on all levels; profound, enthusiastic and physical. Leave it alone, without attempting to get it or break down it or name it. It is essentially all things considered, and can't be found, can't be named and can't be comprehended. It is everything and when you are peacefully, submerged inside yourself, you are there, you are everything and it is you.

## 14- Meditation: Guide for Everybody

Reflection is one of the extraordinary eastern practices that has begun to grab hold in western culture. Truth be told, individuals everywhere throughout the world are profiting by it, both at the top of the priority list and body. Things being what they are, the reason isn't everybody thinking? It may be the case that not every person is aware of all the astounding advantages like expanded unwinding, and diminished degrees of uneasiness and discouragement.

There have been numerous investigations performed on meditation in the most recent decade attempting to comprehend its belongings, just as how it figures out how to help us such a great amount of, both as a main priority for body and soul needs.

The examination into reflection has shown that thinking for a brief timeframe builds alpha waves, which causes us to feel progressively loose, while all the while diminishing our sentiments of uneasiness and discouragement. Alpha waves course through cells in the mind's cortex, where we process tangible data. These waves help smother insignificant or diverting tangible data, permitting us to center. The more alpha waves we have, the better we center.

Through reflection, we increase better fixation, immediacy and inventiveness, satisfaction and true serenity. On-screen characters experience the impacts of reflection on inventiveness direct during acting classes. At whatever point they utilize their imaginative driving forces, they initially think. It might appear to be odd from the outset, yet the outcomes are stunning. Inventiveness floods to the surface once the psyche is freed from the mess.

Reflection can assist us in discovering our motivation throughout everyday life. By turning our consideration inwards, and concentrating absolutely all alone being for extensive stretches of time, contemplation can assist us with increasing another point of view at life, unhindered by our own selfish viewpoint. In the event that you need to pose the philosophical inquiry, "Who am I?" there is no preferable route over through reflection and meditation. At this level, we should begin figuring out how to adopt and adapt a meditation daily practices according to your personal needs.

## 15- Beginning meditation

There is no one-way approach to reflect. As groundwork for the procedure, start by relinquishing any desires you may have. For the initial not many occasions, simply sit easily on the ground, on a pad, or in a seat, and endeavour to relax and calm your brain. You will most likely have numerous contemplations twirling through your head;

about the clothing, super markets, cash, the children, school, the end of the week, and so on. Try not to struggle and battle against your contemplations. They are entirely common. As they cross your thoughts, notice them, acknowledge them, and afterwards delicately bring your concentration and consideration back. You will get a progressively definite clarification in a second. The more you stay aware of your reflection (not at a time, however through a mind-blowing span), the more you can calm your considerations, quiet your brain, and core interest.

Presumably, after meditation sessions you need to know whether you're "doing it right". Most of us feel a similar way. It isn't unexpected to think about whether you are sitting accurately, or breathing effectively, or concentrating on the correct thing. At long last, none of those issues. In the event that you feel better in the wake of ruminating, you're most likely doing it right.

Some people are wondering about meditation hardness. It truly isn't, the length of you don't have any desires going in. Try not to hope to sit in flawless tranquillity your first time through. It's totally fine on the off chance that you don't. Contemplation is for you, and for only you. It is extraordinary for you. Leave it alone whatever it is, only for you.

At this level when you first begin ruminating, you may battle to quiet all the inward babble you have going on in your psyche starting with one second then onto the next. We as a whole encounter this battle. You are not the only one. The stunt isn't to battle against it, however just to acknowledge it as a major aspect of who you are presently, and that you are basically experiencing an individual change. With time, you will figure out how to quiet your brain. There is nothing you have to never really better. There is no compelling reason to attempt to speed things up. On the off chance that you reflect each day, that is sufficient (regardless of whether it's just for ten or fifteen minutes).

## 16- Breathing techniques

This carries us to the most significant thing, relaxation. meditation is all about breathing; breathing is reflection. Breathing is taking in air and afterwards allowing it to out. You take in by getting your stomach. Outbreak happens when your stomach unwinds. The versatility of your lungs and stomach takes them back to a very still position, pushing out the air. Your body does this without anyone else. So, you can continue taking in your rest, yet you can control it to a degree. What we need to do in reflection or profound breathing is moderate the breath down and take in however much air as could reasonably be expected without stressing. You need a full breath, not a stressed breath.

Sitting or lying easily, take moderate, long breaths, yet don't push it. Keep it loose. Inhale just through your nose obviously, on the off chance that you have a cool, mouth-breathing is fine, and some contemplation methods call for exhalation through the mouth. Utilize your typical breath to begin, and continue expanding the length of every breath by taking the air in somewhat more profound with each breath in. While breathing out, do likewise. Slow down the breathe out and attempt to let out the greater part of your breath before breathing in once more. Keep in mind, don't push or strain or control. Simply develop and extend the breath.

The best activity, which likewise helps clear the brain, is to concentrate on your midsection pushing out with each breathes in and pulling in with the breath out directly around and simply under your navel, and furthermore center around the cool sentiment of air entering your noses close to the tip of your nose. Concentrating on these physical sensations will shield you from hanging on excessively long to considerations that go back and forth during the contemplation.

## 17- Soul and mind clearing

Studies claim that we are animals of thought. We think constantly even during sleeping. In any event, while accomplishing something engrossing like viewing a film or conversing with a companion, we may out of nowhere recollect that we left the car unlocked. This is the essence of being human.

In opposition to famous discernment, meditation and profound breathing don't require an unfilled brain. Musings and thoughts will come to you while pondering.

Some may even be rousing. You could get a thought for a hit tune, wherein case, quit contemplating, record the melody, and start once more.

To the sentiment of your midsection rising and falling, the cool air entering your noses. The idea will leave as most likely as it came. What's more, another will enter to be recognized and discharged. This is an automatic procedure. In the event that you stall out on an idea, return to your breath. In the event that it's extremely hard, have a go at tallying your breaths, and afterwards going backwards. In case you're working superbly, you'll never need counting numbers. That is extraordinary. Simply start once more.

When you've been doing this for some time, you will find that the brain does clear, that considerations come less regularly and are of shorter length. You might have the option to have that experience of leaving the body, where you feel precisely as if you are outside of yourself, looking down from above or from over the room at yourself ruminating.

Another experience is of diving deep inside yourself, to feel the focal point of your brain. It's practically similar to a control community, profound inside the cerebrum, where your awareness lives. Be that as it may, it has an inclination that it. It resembles riding in a space container known to mankind of your cognizance.

You can ponder from numerous points of view. You can sit on the floor, on a pad, or in a seat. You can rest, or stand up, or even stroll around! A few priests really ponder while strolling. Spot yourself in completely any position you need that is generally agreeable for you.

On the off chance that you can, inhale utilizing your stomach, which means the air will arrive at the extremely base of your lungs. This is known as diaphragmatic relaxing. It is an incredible instrument for artists. To know whether you're breathing this way, your stomach should push out and afterwards sink back in. You are allowed to inhale anyway you like, however diaphragmatic taking all by itself is extremely unwinding and recuperating. It might appear to be awkward from the start, however as your stomach increments in quality (it's a muscle), it will get simpler. The individuals who practise yoga will be exceptionally acquainted with this type of relaxation. Likewise, on the off chance that you need to see it practically speaking, kids inhale along these lines normally, particularly pampers.

You can work on breathing using your stomach by laying on the ground, setting your hand(s) over your stomach, and attempting to drive your hand up by breathing deeply into your paunch. That will give you a sense for what it feels like, and you would then be able to move your situation as you see fit and attempt to copy it. In any case, don't worry in the event that you can't support it while pondering. Everything will occur time permitting.

In the event that you yawn during meditation, don't stress. It's completely normal. At the point when we do a great deal of profound breathing and enter a casual express, the body yawns normally. Try not to battle it or think ineffectively about your capacity to center.



We have to remember that the training doesn't include really nodding off. You are attempting to stay alarmed and maintain your concentration and consideration. On the off chance that you are dozing, you are doing not one or the other (and you may fall over, except if you're resting). You can't keep your eyes totally open, as a rule, due to residue and so forth, and our eyes normally get dry. You should flicker, at any rate. You may wish to keep your eyes shut, on the grounds that it assists with concentrating on what's going on inside your body. Some meditation styles state to keep the eyes somewhat open and spotlight on a space a couple of crawls before your eyes.



There are various convictions here, and it is muddled whether any method is superior to another. if you hold to specific convictions, at that point holding explicit shapes with your hands, or putting them in various positions, will have various impacts. You are allowed to look around at the different prospects, in case you're intrigued.

The essential methodology is to put your lower arms or the backs of your hands over your knees (in case you're perched on the floor), palms up, thumb and wring-finger contacting. Another mainstream position is to sit with your hands in your lap, making an oval shape. The rear of your correct hand sits in the palm of your left, fingers over fingers, and the two thumbs tenderly touch one another, shaping the oval. Honestly, any position will be perfect to do. Generally, spot your hands on your knees on the off chance that you like. Most like to have the hands looking up.

## 18.3 Select location

Experienced meditators can ponder in an air terminal, a tram station, or any spot-on earth. However, most lean toward a calm, not very brilliant area. Light isn't an issue, yet many locate an obscured or faintly lit room all the more quieting. Obviously, many appreciate doing as such on a stump in the forested areas or a stone on a peak or the sand on the seashore. Whatever the district, total calm (or mitigating music or nature sounds) is ideal.

Pick someplace calm where you won't be upset. Reflection requires delayed center, and if your consideration is continually being hauled somewhere else, it will be hard to do until you have more understanding. With time, your center will arrive at a point where you can think anyplace.

## 18.4 Time selection

Most practitioners and specialists recommend pondering in the first part of the day when our brain is completely alert. It will assist you with focusing, and you'll be less inclined to get lethargic. In the event that it doesn't accommodate your timetable to rehearse toward the beginning of the day, at that point do it at night. Pondering has an excessive number of advantages to maintain a strategic distance from it since you can't do it at the "perfect" time.

Since you've made sense of how your body needs you to sit, and what feels normal to you for your contemplation, we layout the essential strides to make you go. It is expected that you as of now have a period and a spot you will reflect that is peaceful, where you won't be upset.

Set a clock for 10-15 minutes, contingent upon to what extent you need to ruminate for. You ought not to ruminate for longer than 15 minutes for your initial scarcely any occasions. The clock will shield you from being diverted and stressing over the progression of time. Attempt to have a clock that blares tenderly, as you may turn out to be progressively delicate to the commotion.

No extraordinary hardware or equipment is required. All you need is you and a spot to sit or rests. Most ponder staying up with a decent, grounded act. Resting is fine, in spite of the fact that it is anything but difficult to nod off along these lines, and dozing isn't ruminating. Profound breathing isn't a snooze. Not that there's anything amiss with a snooze.

You may like a cushion to sit on. Some meditators want to sit up straight with a decent stance, while others incline toward a divider or pad behind them, and may even ponder in a seat or lounge chair. A few practitioners utilize a level, padded tangle, and on that another pad that is moulded sort of like a chocolate layer cake. Sitting on this pad, with legs crossed on the tangle or in a stooping position, can feel entirely steady and agreeable.

Some demonstration lotus or half lotus (leg over leg with one lower leg on the contrary knee for half lotus or the two lower legs on the contrary knee for full lotus). This isn't simple for some, and even the individuals who can sit along these lines will locate that following a couple of moments the foot gets awkward or nods off. The fundamental things to accomplish in sitting position are comfort, so you are not diverted by distress, and great stance. Whatever position permits this, including resting, is fine.

Candles, incense and music can mitigate stress and upgrade contemplation. In the event that you need music, it is ideal to tune in to something non-melodic, similar to rings or chimes or arbitrary woodwind and nature sounds. Nature sounds, similar to the sea or a stream or downpour can be superb, particularly on the off chance that you live in an urban territory with traffic sounds, alarms, individuals' music, dump trucks, and so on, in light of the fact that the sounds can help quiet the ecological aural mess.

 I utilize a kitchen clock that I got before advanced cells were a thing. I punch in the measure of time I need to reflect (normally 10- 20 minutes, despite the fact that I add a moment to permit myself an opportunity to settle in), and that is it. Why a clock? At that point, you don't have to check the clock. What's more, when you begin, you'll need to check the clock a ton, and when you do, in the wake of feeling like you've contemplated for a half-hour and hope to see it's been under four minutes, you'll see what's so incredible about a clock.

## 19- Step by step conception

Start by concentrating on your breath. Become mindful of how it moves easily all through your body. Concentrate on it, and the focuses where it changes from breathing into breathing out. Envision that your breath is moving all through a structure, its entryway opening in the two headings and never truly shutting.

You will see musings fly into your head once in a while, maybe regularly from the outset. Your psyche has a specific recurring pattern to it. Acknowledge it, and acknowledge yourself. Your brain and body both comprehend what they're doing. Recognize the thought(s), and afterwards, take your concentration back to your breath.

You may check your breath. Start by tallying each breathes in and breathe out as one check, independently. Attempt to get to ten. If your brain strays, begin checking back at one after you've concentrated back on your breath. At the point when you get to ten, start again at one. When you've gotten to ten a couple of times, attempt to tally each breathe in and breathe out together as only one tally. Once more, attempt to get to ten and gradually more and more.

The more frequently you ponder, the more rapidly you will see its benefits. You will see that a little while later, you can without much of a stretch get the chance to reach a stage. You'll likewise see that you get past the means quicker, as you figure out how to center. You may then grow your training by concentrating on a word or slogan or some likeness thereof. Anything you find moving or inspirational is an extraordinary motto to utilize. Rehash the mantra quietly in your mind for the length of your training.

The hardest piece of meditation is staying with it. Numerous individuals get disheartened on the grounds that they believe they "can't do it." To those inclination debilitated, let go of your desires. Without those desires, nobody is making a decision about your contemplation. It is just for yourself and your own benefit. On the off chance that you stick to it for barely any months, you will arrive, ensured.

The sad truth is that while a large portion of people knows about the advantages of meditation, not many of us really have a standard reflection practice. There are a ton of snags to defeat so as to consolidate contemplation into our day to day lives. I conquered those obstructions and have been thinking day by day for a long time just as contemplating occasionally for the duration of the day. Through contemplation, we encounter more harmony and satisfaction in our life. few daily practices may help us to be less receptive and less focused and we gain more vitality and innovativeness. Are you ready? I realize you can encounter these advantages too.

## 20- Meditation Obstacles

### 20.1 lack of time /opportunity and how to fix it

The greatest obstruction individuals face in building up ordinary meditation practices is TIME. people all over the world referenced they need more an ideal opportunity to think and exercise rumination

The normal individual holds up 4-5 hours daily. We sit tight for arrangements, we hold up in rush hour gridlock, we hold up in line at the market and we look out for hang on the telephone. However, those valuable "holding up times" can be changed over into pondering occasions.

So, next time you are sitting tight for an arrangement, pause for a minute to see your breath. Or on the other hand next time you are holding up in line at the supermarket, pause for a minute to grin from within.

Second, have an everyday movement be your reflection. You can fuse contemplation into any of these everyday exercises:

*brushing your teeth

*emptying the dishwasher

*showering

*eating

*walking

*folding clothing, pressing

As you brush your teeth, notice your breath. Or on the other hand, notice the aliveness in your grasp and mouth. As you void the dishwasher, feel the aliveness in your grasp as you set each dish aside.

Third, have your dog or cat be your reflection! Have you at any point seen when strolling your pooch how your canine is totally at the time, taking in its environmental factors? Well, you can join your pooch in this delighted state. When strolling the canine notification, the aliveness in your feet with each progression. Notice the aliveness of the trees, winged animals, your environmental factors.

While petting the feline, notice the non-abrasiveness of the hide. Be totally present with your pooch or feline!

Four, ponder while driving! Presently, obviously, don't close your eyes and ponder while driving. Yet, you can be totally present while driving, with your eyes open. While driving, notice the aliveness in your grasp as you contact the guiding wheel. Or on the other hand at a stop sign or in rush hour gridlock, notice your breath.

These are straightforward ways you can consolidate reflection into your everyday existence without removing anytime from your present calendar. On the off chance that we as a whole did these straightforward things, we'd have a day by day contemplation practice!

## 20.2 Lack of Self-Discipline

One of the greatest hindrance individuals face in consolidating reflection into their everyday life is the absence of self-restraint! Reflection is associated with the discipline. I know a large number of us begin with incredible expectations to ponder day by day or to practice day by day and we may do it for two or three weeks, however then they do not have the ability to control this process for a long time.

So, in the event that you need self-control, discover a reflection helpmate. Ask your life partner, accomplice, companion, colleague to go along with you in joining reflection into your day by day life. Or on the other hand regardless of whether you can't discover somebody that needs to think with you, tell your life partner/companion/accomplice/colleague of your aim to reflect day by day and ask him/her to check in with you and ask you how you are getting along.

## 20.3 Lack of space

The greatest snag individuals referenced isn't having the correct spot or space to think and practise meditation. This is an "apparent hindrance." People can truly think anyplace; while driving a vehicle or strolling through a jam-packed shopping center. Individuals frequently claim the lack of the perfect spot or space to think as a reason to not ruminate. In the event that we consistently trust that the correct conditions will ruminate, we'll never ponder.

We encourage individuals with a reflection task; that is to ponder in an open spot! They can stroll through the divider and notice individuals and spots while watching their breath or seeing the aliveness in their feet.

## 20.4 Interruptions

The most normal grumbling from individuals is that there are such a large number of interruptions to ruminate. In the event that you are pondering and an interruption occurs. Simply notice it. Permit it to be. In the event that it's something that needs your consideration, keep an eye on whatever should be done, while as yet watching your breath.



Such huge numbers of individuals feel that they don't have the foggiest idea of how to meditate. We make the reflection more entangled than it is in reality. Once more, contemplation is tied in with being available at the time. It's extremely about finding what works for you.

Besides, you can consolidate reflection into your existence without removing time from your timetable. Your life can turn into a contemplation. It is those minutes for the duration of the day that we are completely present at the time that issue. Also, through contemplation, we find the joy of being that we are.



Any human being needs to invest an excessive amount of energy on meditation and reflection to create a balance between body and soul. You will discover after a brief timeframe, despite some differences with the individual, that it is anything but difficult to do and that you would prefer not to miss it. Once that occurs, you will comprehend why such huge numbers of individuals worldwide have made meditation part of their everyday schedule, and why such a large number of specialists, advisors and others engaged with physical and passionate wellbeing feel that contemplation is perhaps the most ideal approaches to accomplish genuine health and harmony.

## 22- Recommendations

Another logical truth is that reflection is known to place you into a more profound condition of rest than profound rest. Profound rest is related to a delta brainwave. Profound contemplation can drop you into that delta brainwave quickly, accomplishing the impacts in a shorter measure of time.

For each issue, an answer exists. At the point when your psyche is clear and you're in a condition of harmony, arrangements show up. Being in a condition of harmony just normally draws in arrangements and pathways into your field of view.

In the event that answers for issues show up more much of the time while contemplating day by day, at that point envision what befalls your regular assignments. Answers for regular daily existence become increasingly self-evident. Also, you start to observe these unpretentious changes as your otherworldly vision develops more clear and more extensive.

Talking about pressure, reflection profoundly affects lessening worry in your body. Since contemplation advances harmony and inward quiet, stress breaks down drastically from this reflective procedure.

Reflection is ground-breaking at clearing the brain and concentrating on basic things... like relaxing... or on the other hand a bloom. Be that as it may, it tends to be utilized for quite a lot more. To capably show your wants, you should get away from social turbulence in order to reach the wellspring show of  Universe. On the off chance that your spirits are on high while you envision, at that point, the correspondence channel for showing positive occasions throughout your life is reinforced.

Lastly, when you reflect all the time, you simply feel phenomenal. Easy. You feel better. Everything else is subtleties.

Is it accurate to say that you are searching for a specific cure, for example, diminished nervousness or lower pulse. In spite of the fact that advocates of most meditation practices guarantee medical advantages, as often as possible these cases of advantage refer to logical research that was really led to different types of reflection, and not on the work on being advanced. However, investigate has unmistakably indicated that not all contemplations give the equivalent results. In case you're picking a reflection method for a particular medical advantage, check the examination being utilized and confirm that a specific advantage was really done on that particular reflection procedure and not on some other practice. While you are investigating the exploration, be certain the examination was peer-checked on and distributed in a respectable logical or scholastic diary. In the event that an examination indicating a particular advantage, for example, profound unwinding or diminished tension was duplicated by a few other research concentrates on that equivalent practice, at that point the science is additionally convincing.

With regards to diminishing pressure and uneasiness, researchers have again discovered that all contemplation practices are not similarly compelling. Practices that utilize focus have been found to really build nervousness, and the equivalent meta-study found that most reflection procedures are not any more powerful than a fake treatment at diminishing anxiety.

The Supernatural Reflection method is the main psyche/body practice that has been indicated both in autonomous clinical preliminaries and meta-investigations to fundamentally bring down hypertension in hypertensive patients. To decide whether a specific type of contemplation has logical proof supporting a particular advantage, you can do some research. There are over a thousand companion inspected concentrates on the different types of reflection, with the Supernatural Contemplation strategy and care reflection being the most widely inquired about practices, separately.